CW00493791

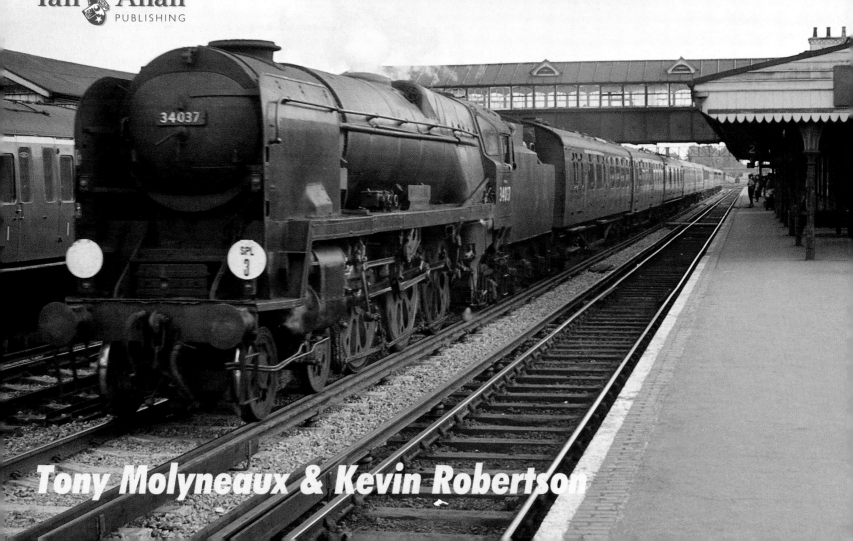

THE HEYDAY OF EASTLEIGH and its LOCOMOTIVES

Ian Allan PUBLISHING

34037

Tony Molyneaux & Kevin Robertson

Front cover: 'S15' 4-6-0 No 30828 (nowadays the pride of the Eastleigh Railway Preservation Society), seen here near Chandlers Ford with an Eastleigh-bound goods. The smart piece of what appears to be agricultural equipment (red) contrasts with the work-stained vans, while the locomotive itself could also benefit from the attention of the cleaners.

Back cover: Eastleigh shed, or MPD, to give its more correct title at the time this view was recorded. (It was always known as 'The Shed' to generations of spotters.) 'Battle of Britain' No 34064 *Fighter Command*, fitted with a Giesl oblong ejector, poses by the coal stage in the evening sun of a late-winter's day, 17 March 1962. The locomotive was then based at Exmouth Junction and was visiting Eastleigh for servicing before working back to its home shed. Such variety of machinery understandably made Eastleigh a Mecca for enthusiasts from both near and far.

Title page: AWS-fitted rebuilt 'West Country' No 34037 *Clovelly* with what is recorded as 'empties' for an ocean-liner service (yet displaying an inter-regional headcode) on 7 July 1967. The locomotive is unusual in retaining its nameplates, as by this time most of these had been removed to prevent pilfering. The location is the north end of Eastleigh station; the works and shed, situated to the south of the complex, will be seen in later views. The presence of the 'juice' rails will be noted. No 34037 had been rebuilt in the form seen here at Eastleigh in March 1958.

First published 2005

ISBN 0 7110 3088 X

All rights reserved. No part of this book may be reproduced or transmitted in any form or by any means, electronic or mechanical, including photocopying, recording or by any information storage and retrieval system, without permission from the Publisher in writing.

© Ian Allan Publishing Ltd 2005

Published by Ian Allan Publishing

an imprint of Ian Allan Publishing Ltd, Hersham, Surrey KT12 4RG.
Printed in England by Ian Allan Printing Ltd, Hersham, Surrey KT12 4RG.

Code: 0506/B2

Introduction

The Heyday of Eastleigh and its Locomotives is a title open to a degree of differing interpretation. According to the viewpoint of the individual it could refer to the locomotives built and repaired at Eastleigh, stabled and allocated at Eastleigh, or even operating from and through Eastleigh. All would be correct, dependent upon choice and perspective, but in the theme for this book the principle has been the classes that were based at and visited the Hampshire works and shed.

Hampshire itself is, of course, primarily a rural county, in which, compared with the counties of the Midlands and the North, industry has understandably been sparse. Yet at Eastleigh, in 1910, on what had been a greenfield site, Dugald Drummond established for the then London & South Western Railway a locomotive- and carriage-building/repair complex which would eventually become the principal works of its successors the Southern Railway and British Railways Southern Region. That position would endure until the 1960s, after which various changes in policy as well as operational requirements would see considerable contraction. Sadly at the end of 2004 it was announced by the current owners that the former locomotive works would close by the end of 2005, thereby meeting a fate similar to that suffered by its one-time counterpart on the GWR at Swindon, which finally closed its doors some 20 years ago.

Whilst Eastleigh and Swindon may have been established by different (and, let it also be said, rival) companies, there was some similarity with regard to the choice of site, each being at a junction location and each a similar distance from the main London terminus of the railway concerned. The dark days of the 1940s witnessed a first sharing of some production between the two sites, which would later be developed further under British Railways, as work originating on one region was given to a works on another, in order to maintain employment as well as to ensure stock was not standing idle awaiting repair for longer than was necessary.

But to return to the origins of Eastleigh and the shed complex itself. This had existed in its remembered form since 1903 and was a direct replacement for the locomotive shed at Northam, which had served Southampton, as well as an existing small two-road shed at Eastleigh station. One can only imagine the effect such a colossus must have had on the area. Eastleigh was now well and truly on the map, both locomotive and carriage construction being transferred from the cramped site at Nine Elms in South West London to a location where the new shed afforded the opportunity not only to service the needs from an operational perspective but also to store engines awaiting works attention as well as those based temporarily at Eastleigh and needing to be 'run in', having been newly built or repaired.

Eastleigh would continue to perform its multiple role throughout the steam era, which itself finally came to an end on 9 July 1967; demolition of the steam shed began the very next day, those men who remained (albeit in different roles) recalling a firm instruction to clear everything out by midnight on 9 July, otherwise it would be in the hands of the demolition contractors.

For some 60 years Eastleigh shed (or, in BR parlance, Motive Power Depot) performed the role of supplying locomotives for trains to a variety of locations both on and off the Southern system. Eastleigh men and machines worked a number of diagrams, to destinations as diverse as Weymouth, Waterloo, Salisbury, Chichester, Banbury, Newbury and Guildford. Eastleigh men thus had some of the widest route knowledge there was and were often supplemented by men transferred from other depots, who in turn brought with them additional skills. It was a roster clerk's delight and meant that junior men arriving on promotion could often find themselves working trains which would normally have been far beyond their usual link, simply because of their additional route knowledge. For many years Eastleigh was also responsible for locomotives at the sub-sheds of Andover Junction, Lymington, Southampton Terminus and Winchester City, to which Eastleigh men sometimes found themselves on temporary transfer to cover for holidays and/or sickness.

As far as local duties were concerned the depot would supply motive power for most of the boat trains to/from Southampton Docks, which until the advent of the jet age was the principal transatlantic port. By the end of the 1950s all of the 'Lord Nelson' class had arrived at Eastleigh and aside from boat trains would also see employment on the various semi-fast services operating on the Bournemouth line. This did not stop temporary transfers between depots on occasions, and it was not unknown for a harassed shed foreman to 'borrow' an engine from another depot to cover a particular duty.

From the perspective of variety the heyday of Eastleigh and its locomotives could really be said to be the late 1950s and early 1960s, and where possible it is from this period that the illustrations in this book have been chosen; the subsequent influx of locomotives displaced (by electrification) from the Eastern section resulted in a mass exodus of older types, and by 1967 main-line steam traction was reduced to the surviving Bulleid Pacifics and a number of Standard types.

Tony Molyneaux was fortunate to have been able to record the scene around Eastleigh from the late 1950s onwards, and to afford variety in the illustrations a number of views have been chosen to show Eastleigh-based types on duties within a reasonable radius. I must confess that this latter decision was due partly to my having been captivated by the quality of a number of the views chosen, and it is a pity there is only a finite number of pages available, the finished product being of necessity a compromise of machines, locations and dates.

I am as ever grateful to Tony for making his collection freely available both to myself, in so far as the selection of illustrations is concerned, and ultimately to the wider readership. To the best of our knowledge none of the pictures selected has previously been published, and it is thus a privilege to act as the compiler of what is both a nostalgic and unique volume.

Kevin Robertson
Eastleigh
April 2005

Above: We commence our look at Eastleigh and its locomotives some 15 miles to the north, where the tunnels at Micheldever were near the start of the long 1-in-250 downhill gradient, which continued as far south as Eastleigh. Rebuilt 'West Country' No 34001 *Exeter* is on Bournemouth duty No 428, which should see the train pass through Eastleigh in little more than 15 minutes' time. The date is 2 September 1961, and the stock seemingly exclusively to Maunsell design.

Right: Another down express hurrying south on 2 September 1961, this time with 'Battle of Britain' No 34052 *Lord Dowding* in charge. The photograph was taken from the down platform loop, the up and down through lines then being devoid of a platform face. This situation would change a few years later when, as a result of electrification, a single island platform was provided and the loops were removed, while the signalbox would close in 1966 with the advent of the Eastleigh and Basingstoke multiple-aspect signalling (MAS) schemes.

Left: Bournemouth duty No 433 would normally involve a 'Merchant Navy' locomotive working the 1.12pm Waterloo–Weymouth service. On 2 September 1961, however, no doubt due to non-availability, 'West Country' No 34016 *Bodmin* was in charge and appears to be working well just south of Micheldever on its way towards Winchester and Eastleigh, which it would pass non-stop, Southampton being the first scheduled call. The set number (292) applied to the first six vehicles in the train, which were formed as a permanently coupled Bulleid kitchen/restaurant-car rake.

Above: At a slightly more sedate pace and sadly also nearing the end of its working life, 'King Arthur' No 30770 *Sir Prianius* is working a Basingstoke–Bournemouth stopper, which this time will call at Eastleigh. The view was recorded on 2 September 1961, by which time the locomotive had just over 14 months of active life left, yet the standard of presentation is notable and contrasts with the abject filth that characterised steam in the very last years at Eastleigh and elsewhere.

7

Left: A down boat train with passengers for the *Mauretania* recorded just north of Winchester on 9 September 1961, with rebuilt 'Battle of Britain' No 34077 *603 Squadron* in charge. This would have been an Eastleigh turn, the men working up to Waterloo, possibly 'on the cushions', in order to work the train back. The coaching stock is also somewhat varied, Maunsell and Bulleid designs being supplemented by two Pullman cars at the rear, the formation made up thus so that any VIPs would not have to walk any distance when boarding the train at Waterloo.

Above: 'Battle of Britain' No 34064 *Fighter Command* just north of Winchester on a down express, passing what is still known today as 'The Baltic' siding. The origins of the name are said to go back some 80 years, to the days when a troop platform had existed hereabouts from which soldiers and supplies were despatched to that part of the globe. Note the box containing the batteries for the locomotive's Automatic Warning System (AWS), visible on the front framing just above the buffer-beam.

Above left: The summer of 1965 — 7 July, to be exact — and a rather grubby rebuilt 'Battle of Britain', No 34053 *Sir Keith Park*, approaches Winchester with a down freight bound for the yards at Eastleigh. Although the Bulleid Pacifics frequently undertook freight duties on the West of England line it was somewhat unusual to see one so employed on the Bournemouth line south of Basingstoke. No 34053 was by now in far-from-pristine condition and would be withdrawn just three months later, spending its last days on Southern metals in repose outside the front of Eastleigh shed before finally being towed away to South Wales for scrap. However, it would ultimately escape this fate; rescued from Dai Woodham's yard in 1984, it currently awaits restoration at a private site in Kent.

Left: Also in grubby condition but entrusted to the prestigious 'Pines Express', 'West Country' No 34047 *Callington* slows for the Winchester stop on the same

date, 7 July 1965. Notice the conductor rail off-loaded between the metals of the up line and also the yellow 'dummy' and open-air ground frame; the yellow indication meant a driver could pass the signal for the purpose of shunting. Today the area once occupied by the goods yard on the up side of the line is given over to car parking.

Above: 'B4' 0-4-0T No 30102 in the process of using the down main line for shunting mineral wagons at Winchester on 28 April 1962. This particular locomotive shared the task of shunting here with sister engine No 30096, each being based at Winchester for around one week before returning to Eastleigh for servicing. For many years the regular Winchester driver was a former senior main-line driver who had a prosthetic leg, whilst a number of young Eastleigh firemen had their first experience of the footplate on one of the two 'B4s'.

11

Above: In the 1950s and 1960s a number of LMS-designed (Ivatt) 2-6-2T locomotives were based at Eastleigh, their duties ranging from local passenger services, on which they provided a welcome (and modern) change from the elderly 'M7s', to engineers' trains and shunting turns. No 41305 was recorded on 7 September 1961 on an engineers' train, being seen just south of Shawford Junction as it heads the last few miles back to the yards at Eastleigh.

Right: The standard goods locomotive for the Southern Railway and BR Southern Region in the days of steam was the 'S15' 4-6-0, the origins of which may be traced back to the time of Robert Urie and the LSWR. No 30498 was one of the original batch of five engines ordered in 1916 and built at Eastleigh in the early part of 1920 and would ultimately put in 43 years of useful service, surviving until June 1963. Displaying the Waterloo–Southampton Terminus headcode, the locomotive was photographed at the same location and on the same date as No 41305 in the previous view.

Left: Redundant on the South Eastern section following electrification of the Kent lines, the 'Schools' 4-4-0s were cascaded westward for their final years and became a regular sight on the Lymington boat trains, but on 9 June 1962 (and slightly unusually for the period) Eastleigh turned out a rather grimy BR Class 5, No 73110 *The Red Knight*.

Below: For a brief period in the early 1960s 'Schools' 4-4-0s were a pleasing sight in active service on the Bournemouth line, which situation pertained until the end of 1962; despite the fact that withdrawals had commenced during the previous year the survivors were still entrusted with main-line work throughout their final summer. An example is No 30902 *Wellington*, in reasonably clean condition and in marked contrast with No 73110 in the previous view. The scene was also recorded on 9 June 1962 and again depicts a Waterloo–Lymington turn, the number of similar workings per day giving some idea of the popularity of the service at this time.

Far left: One of the easily recognisable 'Q1' 0-6-0s, No 33023, heads for Southampton with a van train on 9 June 1962. The 'Q1s' could run fast when required and were well capable of the work asked of them — provided the train was fitted, as here. The service has been routed via the down through line rather than the relief, suggesting that the driver was indeed 'getting a move on'. The location is Shawford Cutting, just south of Shawford station (from where there were four tracks as far as the south end of Eastleigh station) and one of Tony's favoured venues, 'Bowkers Footbridge' providing an excellent vantage-point from which to record the passing scene.

Above: Running well through Shawford Cutting and heading south on 1 June 1963 is 'Battle of Britain' No 34064 *Fighter Command*, with not a hint of steam escaping from anywhere it shouldn't (although perhaps this would not be too visible on a summer's day anyway!). No 34064 was always popular with crews, being considered the equal of a 'Merchant Navy', due to the fitting of a Giesl ejector in place of the more usual Bulleid blastpipe and chimney. Plans for a number of other un-rebuilt members of the class to be so equipped were ultimately vetoed by BR on cost grounds, as the life of the steam engine was considered limited. One other Bulleid locomotive — 'West Country' No 34092 *City of Wells* — would subsequently be fitted with a similar device, albeit in preservation.

Right: When not in use on boat-train specials the 'Lord Nelson' 4-6-0s would find themselves 'borrowed' for use on certain inter-regional workings, such as this Bournemouth–Newcastle express (composed of ex-LNER stock) on 29 July 1961. Seen taking the up through line at Otterbourne, just south of Shawford, No 30860 *Lord Hawke* would most likely haul the train as far as Oxford.

Above: Prestige duty for 'Lord Nelson' 4-6-0 No 30856 *Lord St. Vincent* just north of Allbrook on 25 July 1961. Allbrook down signals can be seen on the gantry behind the train, whilst Allbrook itself was — and still is — the northernmost limit of the Eastleigh yard complex. The service is a boat train from Southampton, complete with 'Statesman' headboard, and consists of two vans for luggage at the front and a rake of seven or eight Pullman cars, followed by at least one other luggage van. All-up weight would thus be in the order of 450+ tons, and hauling the train up the gradient for the next 15 miles to the summit at Litchfield would be no mean feat. No wonder there is evidence of firing taking place, although the grey smoke does indicate good combustion.

Right: In any picture book where the choice of views has of necessity to be restricted (for no other reason than space constraints) it is important to strike a balance between the typical and the unusual; moreover, care must be taken not to portray the latter as if it were the norm. Here, then, is an example of the unusual (for the period, at least), as 'Britannia' 4-6-2 No 70004 *William Shakespeare* heads north between Eastleigh and Allbrook with a Southampton Docks–Crewe van train on 17 August 1966. 'Britannias' had been semi-regular visitors to the area in the 1950s but by this time were rare indeed, except on railtour workings. Notice also the mix of mechanical and multiple-aspect signalling, the Eastleigh area being converted to full MAS with effect from 6 November 1966.

Left: For light- and medium-weight freight turns Eastleigh had at its disposal a number of 'N'- and 'U'-class 2-6-0s, the latter generally used for passenger turns, as they possessed slightly larger driving wheels. On 23 May 1962, however, 'U' No 31611 was in charge of a freight, being seen heading north from Allbrook with a train which includes a number of oil tanks suitably marshalled away from the engine.

Above: Seen on a main-line working just south of Allbrook signalbox, BR Class 5 No 73119 *Elaine* slows for the Eastleigh stop on 22 April 1962. The train is recorded as the 11.30 Waterloo–Bournemouth, although the headcode suggests it may be terminating at Southampton. The four arms on the signal gantry were controlled from Allbrook 'box and (from left to right) are: No 8 up local starter, No 4 (short post) up local to up through starter, No 9 (short post) up through to up local starter, No 3 up through starter.

Above: Eastleigh station on 29 May 1965, with 'Battle of Britain' 4-6-2 No 34082 *615 Squadron* entering the station under Bishopstoke Road bridge and passing the massive Eastleigh East signalbox, which had something in the order of 139 levers. The train is a freight, probably bound for Southampton Docks, and is drawing into what was then Platform 3, possibly to allow a faster service to overtake on the through line.

Above right: Busy times at Eastleigh on 15 June 1961, with three of the four main lines occupied. 'Merchant Navy' No 35019 *French Line CGT* has charge of the down 'Bournemouth Belle', passing on the down through, as 'Lord Nelson' No 30857 *Lord Howe* waits to follow with the 2.5pm Eastleigh–Bournemouth West.

Right: Eastleigh's importance as a rail centre extended beyond the station and shed/works complex to include the yards, which constituted one of the principal collection/despatch points for goods to/from other major yards, both on the SR and beyond. Among the most regular freight workings were those to/from Feltham, which for many years were in the hands of 'S15' 4-6-0s. Built at Eastleigh in 1927, No 30830 is seen arriving at the east yard (north of the station) from Feltham on 15 June 1964.

23

Left: One of Tony's earliest colour slides is this view from 12 October 1956 depicting No 73117 at Eastleigh's Platform 3 with a down Bournemouth service. Both this train and that waiting at the up platform are formed (in part, at least) of Bulleid stock painted in the contemporary red and cream. All SR locomotive-hauled stock would later revert to green.

Above: More busy times at Eastleigh, this time almost a decade later, on 29 May 1965. 'West Country' No 34103 *Calstock* is about to depart with the 10.15 freight to Salisbury, whilst the tender of another Bulleid type can just be seen attached to the train at Platform 2.

Left: 'S15' No 30496, dating from 1921, is seemingly struggling a bit as it passes through Eastleigh on the down through line on 24 March 1962. The Urie-designed members of the class would all be withdrawn between November 1962 and April 1964, this particular locomotive being one of the early casualties, succumbing in January 1963.

Above: The other Winchester shunter (page 11 refers). In the spring of 1963 'B4' No 30096 leaves the works yard with an LCGB special which had originated at Winchester Chesil and made its way to Southampton Docks and was returning to Winchester City via Eastleigh Works. In the background can be seen two motor coaches from 'Hampshire' DEMU sets, whilst the signals are those controlling exit from the Fareham/Gosport route onto the main line.

27

Left: Ivatt 2-6-2 tank (or, as the type was also known, 'Mickey Mouse') No 41298 was regularly employed on shunting the east yard after the demise of the 'Z' class. The Ivatt design, whilst certainly lacking the all-out power of a 'Z', was more versatile in that could also be used on local passenger work when required; on 16 July 1965 this example was in charge of the 19.52 local to Southampton, the train comprising two Mk 1s and a Bulleid brake.

Above: Rear view of a Drummond-designed '700'-class locomotive, No 30315, running southwards on the through road with a steam crane and mess van in August 1959. Tony's records refer to this as a permanent-way working, although no information can be gleaned from the picture itself.

Above: 'And now for something completely different ……' Urie 'H16' 4-6-2T No 30516 and an unidentified 'Q'-class 0-6-0 and 4-6-0 stand on the up through line at Eastleigh on 21 May 1960. The combination is unusual, to say the least, and it is not certain whether all the locomotives are actually in steam. If not (as seems likely), one or more could be destined for a works visit; otherwise the probable destination is the east yard, where all three will be routed onto waiting trains.

Right: Non-stop through Eastleigh. 'Merchant Navy' No 35027 *Port Line* runs past its birthplace on 29 May 1965 with the 10.30 from Weymouth to Waterloo.

Above: The final days of steam. With coal piled high on the tender, having just come off shed ready for duty, 'West Country' No 34021, formerly named *Dartmoor*, stands alongside Platform 3 on Friday 7 July 1967. From this time Southern steam had but two days to go — note the presence of the new 'TC' sets in the carriage sidings alongside the Portsmouth line.

Right: Contrasting with the grimy appearance of the Pacific in the previous view, Ivatt Class 2 No 41314 looks positively pristine as it stands in the west yard at Eastleigh some five years earlier, on 24 June 1962. The buildings in the background were part of the Carriage Works complex, which moved to Eastleigh in 1891.

Moving now towards the shed area, and on 9 September 1961 'Battle of Britain' No 34051 *Winston Churchill* stands outside the shed, apparently ex works and presumably awaiting a running-in turn. The piles of ash and clinker visible in the foreground were an all-too-common feature of the busy steam shed. Alongside the locomotive is one of the packing/mess vans from the breakdown train. In the background can be seen the water tank atop the former dormitory and office block, whilst the signal at the end of the building was operated solely for the purpose of testing the eyesight of footplate crews.

Another clean and possibly ex-works engine, 'U'-class 2-6-0 No 31639, after what was probably its final works visit, in a photograph taken on 6 June 1963. Visible in the background is the Works itself, separated from the shed by a public road lined with trees. Notice too (on the locomotive's smoke-deflector) the electrification 'flash', by then applied as standard to all steam engines, although it is doubtful whether by this time any Southern machines actually ventured into areas where overhead wires posed a danger.

As mentioned in the Introduction, following the Grouping Eastleigh took over as the premier works on the SR system, with the result that there were regular visits from engines whose pedigree had been established elsewhere. Such was the case on 26 August 1961, when ex-LBSCR 'K'-class 2-6-0 No 32353 was recorded alongside the coal stack at the rear of the steam shed. This stockpile, consisting of hundreds of tons, was intended as an emergency supply, the task of stacking usually being performed by shed labourers and cleaners.

Variations in livery and cleanliness at the rear of the shed on 10 November 1963.
BR Standard Class 4 tank No 80140 appears in good external condition, as does the
green 'USA' tank behind, whilst No 31631 was likewise in 'reasonable nick'. Sadly,
as time passed these would be the exceptions, and the general rule became more like
the unidentified machines in the background.

Above left: On a murky 12 August 1962 — a matter of weeks from the end of its active service — 'Lord Nelson' No 30857 *Lord Howe* awaits its next duty outside the front of the shed. The locomotive was probably being prepared for a boat train to or from Southampton, upon which work it would remain until the end of the summer timetable and with it the end of a career of nearly 34 years.

Left: A 'Nelson' at Eastleigh in August 1959, No 30858 *Lord Duncan* apparently being shunted at the rear of the shed by 'E4' 0-6-2T No 32510. A number of 'E4s' were based at Eastleigh and together with the 'USA' 0-6-0Ts found employment in the docks at Southampton until ousted by diesel shunters from 1962 onwards.

Above: Fresh from overhaul, rebuilt 'Merchant Navy' No 35022 *Holland-America Line* stands at the rear of Eastleigh shed on 12 August 1962, awaiting running-in before returning to its home depot of Exmouth Junction. The restored 'T9' No 120 will also be noted behind. Eastleigh never had a regular allocation of 'Merchant Navy' locomotives, although all members of the class visited the shed, having been built, rebuilt and overhauled at the nearby Works.

A definite poser. 'West Country' No 34044 *Woolacombe* poses in the evening sun
at Eastleigh on 6 June 1963 with obviously red coupling rods, the most likely
explanation being over-exuberance on the part of a painter!

An engine at the end of its life. Adams radial tank No 30582 stands on the scrap road at Eastleigh, with what appears to be an Ashford 'C' class behind. This view was recorded in August 1961, one month after No 30582 and sister engine No 30583 had been withdrawn. No 30583 was destined to survive, however, and currently resides on the Bluebell Railway in East Sussex.

42 As well as playing host to SR and BR types Eastleigh enjoyed regular visits from WR and LMR machines, while in the early 1950s it was possible to see locomotives emanating from the Eastern Region, when ex-LNER 'V2' 2-6-2s had stood in to cover for the temporary withdrawal of the Bulleid Pacifics. On 5 July 1961 ex-GWR '73xx' Mogul, No 7332, waits to return to the Western Region, having deposited its train in the east yard, the 7.07pm arrival from Oxford which service had originated as the 12.15pm from Washford Heath. It was common practice at this time for a well turned out WR engine to be in charge of this working from Hinksey, south of Oxford, and which ran via Newbury.

A visitor from the South Eastern section, in the form of Brighton-built Fairburn
2-6-4T No 42082, stands in front of 'U'-class 2-6-0 No 31792 in August 1959.
This view also affords a glimpse into the shed itself, the glass front of which
had been replaced in early BR days by the corrugated panels seen here.

26 August 1962 was no doubt a busy day for the shed, for 'King Arthur' No 30770 *Sir Prianius* is the only engine visible as it sets off for work. This particular machine had been built for the Southern Railway by the North British Locomotive Co in 1925 and survived until November 1962, by which time it had covered just over 1.1 million miles.

The end of the road for 'W' class 2-6-4T No 31915, already rusting at Eastleigh on 10 November 1963, having been withdrawn only the previous month. Nine of the class ended their days at Eastleigh and were broken up at the neighbouring works; the shed itself witnessed only a limited amount of cutting-up and then mainly in the very last days of steam.

Above: A 'G6' 0-6-0, now renumbered DS682, in store alongside the new diesel shed at Eastleigh on 3 March 1963. Previously numbered 30238, it had been transferred to service stock in 1960 and worked as such until withdrawn in December 1962. When photographed it too was awaiting a call to the scrapyard at the rear of the Works.

Above right: Associated with Eastleigh for over 60 years were the 'M7' 0-4-4Ts, used on local passenger-services within Hampshire. Such was their longevity that a number even survived the 'dieselisation' of a number of branch services from 1957

onwards. Seen ex works at Eastleigh on 17 March 1962, No 30045 retains its Westinghouse pump and push-pull fittings.

Right: Another candidate on the scrap line, this time on 14 October 1962, was Ashford-built 'H'-class 0-4-4T No 31278, which had been condemned that very month. To the right of the locomotive is the bunker of what appears to be an 'M7', which may well be awaiting the same fate. Not so, however, 'S15' No 30832 (left), which was destined to survive until January 1964.

Above left: 'Soled and heeled' was the term given to a heavy intermediate overhaul, which usually involved only a partial repaint, as in the case of BR Standard Class 4 4-6-0 No 75074, seen just off the turntable at Eastleigh. The shed was provided with a triangle forming a connection with the Portsmouth line so that engines did not have to queue to turn and thus relieving what would otherwise have been a congestion point.

Left: Fresh from overhaul but seemingly not required for work at present, judging by the rust on its wheels, Standard Class 4 4-6-0 No 75030 is seen on 11 September 1965 outside the shed, which was also playing host to an LMS-designed Class 4 2-6-0, No 43155.

Above: The use of the big 'Z'-class tank engines as yard shunters at Eastleigh has already been mentioned, although by the end of 1962 this had ceased and the entire class of eight had been withdrawn. They were incredibly powerful and on banking duties (such as at Exeter) were without equal in steam days; as yard shunters, however, they were not so popular, being considered somewhat clumsy machines. Its working days now over, No 30955 stands on the scrap road at Eastleigh shed on 3 March 1963.

Above: A bright spot in the ever-increasing pace of decline in steam working through the 1960s was the restoration of 'T9' No 30120 to LSWR livery in 1963, its survival guaranteed as part of the national collection; the locomotive was then used on a number of enthusiast specials. Seen at Eastleigh on 3 March 1963, it provides a marked contrast in condition with the rebuilt 'West Country' behind.

Above right: Another engine with red coupling rods (see page 40), this time 'Terrier' No DS680, recorded in March 1963, by which date it had been displaced from its role as Lancing Carriage Works shunter by a 'USA' 0-6-0 tank. In the background can be seen the front of the new diesel shed, erected initially to service the 'Hampshire' DEMUs; much extended in later years, it still stands today.

Right: Somewhat modified from its original form, this ex-LSWR 'Ironclad' displays a smart new red livery as part of the Eastleigh breakdown train, photographed on 7 October 1962. In common with the depots at Guildford, Salisbury and Bournemouth, Eastleigh maintained its own breakdown crane and associated gang, the men being drawn from a pool of artisans in the shed and on call '24/7' to deal with any untoward incidents in their immediate area as well as assisting elsewhere as required.

Above left: Travelling by train between Winchester and Southampton for school, the writer regarded a look at the comings and goings at Eastleigh shed as a 'must' at the end of each day, but nothing could have prepared him for the sight which greeted him on the morning of 24 April 1964. Photographed later the same day, ex-LNER 'A4' No 60008 *Dwight D. Eisenhower* stands outside the front of the shed *en route* to Southampton and a passage across the Atlantic to preservation in the USA.

Left: Another incidence of the unusual, as a very grimy 'USA' No 30067 shunts a one-time GWR pannier tank, now renumbered L90 in the ownership of London

Transport. The latter locomotive was one of several of its type operated by London Transport, Eastleigh being charged with undertaking repairs and overhauls when necessary. This would be one of the last major steam repairs carried out by the Hampshire works, the date being 19 September 1965.

Above: Out to grass. Radial tank No 30584 and 'T9' No 30287 await the call to the scrapyard outside the back of the shed, while standing alongside is a visitor from the WR in the form of 'Hall' 4-6-0 No 4914 *Cranmore Hall*. The date is 9 September 1961, and the mass slaughter of ex-LSWR types is underway.

Left: Thus far the scenes depicted have been confined to the shed and its immediate environs. However, as Eastleigh was also home to the principal locomotive works on the Southern Region it is appropriate now to include some photographs taken therein. On 24 October 1959 'M7' No 30241 was in the course of overhaul, resplendent in new paint but still waiting for its chimney (amongst other parts) to be replaced. Sister locomotive No 30378 is evidently alongside, the number conveniently chalked on the bunker.

Above: During the summer and autumn of 1959 it could almost be believed that Eastleigh was concentrating solely on 'M7'-class repairs and overhauls, and indeed this was not far from the truth as members of the class were given an extended lease of life due to teething troubles with the new diesel units. Here Nos 30245 and 30029 are receiving attention, whilst at the rear is a third, unidentified member of the class, with two Standard designs also visible on the left.

Above: As well as undertaking repairs on certain London Transport locomotives Eastleigh Works carried out major overhauls on some of the Longmoor Military Railway machines. Freshly outshopped in LMR blue, 2-10-0 No 601 *Kitchener* makes a splendid sight posed outside the front of the works on 14 September 1963.

Right: Seen on the same date and at the same location is Standard Class 5 4-6-0 No 73049. The absence of any white paint on the smokebox numberplate will be noted. Some crews preferred the Class 5 locomotives to the Bulleid breed, the BR type being considered strong and reliable, albeit somewhat rough-riding.

Above left: Leaving Eastleigh, we now head southwards past the complex of sidings at Stoneham, which were laid in wartime to afford a place for locomotive storage away from the main shed area visible in the background; later this location would be used to join together sections of conductor rail laid in 1965/6, using a mobile welding plant borrowed from London Transport. The train, bound for Fawley, consists of empty tankers which would most likely have arrived at Eastleigh via the Didcot, Newbury & Southampton line behind a Class 9F ('92xxx') locomotive; however, these were barred from the Fawley branch, so trains between Eastleigh and Fawley were invariably worked by tank engines (there being no turntable at Fawley). A regular Eastleigh engine, Ivatt Class 2 No 41329 is seen at the head of a long rake on 17 May 1962.

Left: Another type which for long featured on the Fawley empties was the 'W' 2-6-4T class. No 31916 seen with the 6.55pm from Eastleigh on 29 June 1961, complete with obligatory barrier wagons.

Above: The evening sun catches 'U'-class 2-6-0 No 31794 as it passes Stoneham sidings with a Bournemouth-line stopper on 6 June 1962. The locomotive was one of a number that had started life as tank engines of the 'River' class, although all had been rebuilt in the form seen here long before the advent of BR.

Above: A final view at Stoneham (and proving that not just Fawley trains passed that way), with 'Lord Nelson' 4-6-0 No 30864 *Sir Martin Frobisher* in charge of the down 'Holland-America' boat train on 19 July 1961. Headboards were not always carried on these services, hampering identification. The headboards for the boat trains were stored at the front of Eastleigh steam shed at one end of an old coach body which was also used as the Mutual Improvement classroom and ambulance room.

Right: Another boat train, this time the down 'Statesman' on 26 April 1967 — some years after the demise of the 'Lord Nelsons'. Accordingly a 'West Country' is in charge, No 34013 *Okehampton* running through the new station at Southampton Airport (later designated 'Parkway'), seen here in original form before the expansion of later years.

Left: Dating from the 1880s, Swaythling station had been built in the belief that eventually four tracks would be provided south of Eastleigh, and accordingly the main buildings were set back to allow for an expansion which was destined never to happen. 'West Country' No 34020 *Seaton* was recorded on 31 July 1960 at the head of a typical Bournemouth-line working of the 1960s, the 1.30pm from Waterloo.

Below left: The next station was at St Denys, where the four platforms were split — two for main-line services and two curving away on the Netley line. This was the scene on 17 July 1965, with a rather grimy 'Merchant Navy', No 35027 *Port Line*, in charge of the up 'Pines Express', which it would haul as far as Oxford, running via the Reading West curve. At the time this was one of the few regular workings for maroon coaching stock on the SR.

Right: South of St Denys there was another section of four-track main line as far as Northam Junction, 'Battle of Britain' No 34055 *Fighter Pilot* being seen with a Southampton Terminus train on the down slow route just south of the station. In the days of BR steam the sand-drag (left) was the scene of two incidents whereby Bulleid Pacifics failed to stop, ending up on 'Olde England'. Pictured on 12 April 1963, No 34055 was not one of those involved, although it would have the dubious distinction of being the first to be withdrawn, just 10 days later, when it failed near Chichester with a cracked inside cylinder, major repairs to steam locomotives not being warranted by this time. The same reason would be used to justify the withdrawal of a number of the Bulleid Pacifics as the months and years progressed.

Left: Southampton Central in the process of transition on 11 April 1966. The clock tower is still extant but will shortly be demolished to make way for the new concrete station, whilst 'pots' are present on the sleepers ready to receive conductor rail. For the time being, however, steam still remains supreme, with 'Battle of Britain' No 34066 *Spitfire* ready to leave with the 14.00 service to Waterloo. The white-painted hinges to the smokebox door were a feature of a number of the last engines working from Eastleigh in 1966/7.

Right: Almost 10 years earlier, and another of Tony's early slides. 'U'-class 2-6-0 No 31807 waits just outside Southampton Central on 7 January 1957 with the stock for the 11.30am service from Southampton to Portsmouth via Netley.

Above: A hot summer's day, and a locomotive that has recently become rather hot as well, judging by the scorchmarks on the side of the firebox casing. No 34064 *Fighter Command* leaves Southampton westwards in August 1966, hauling a mixed rake of Bulleid and BR Standard coaches. By this time restricted maintenance applied not only to locomotive stock; coaches too were being withdrawn almost on an *ad hoc* basis, a number of sets being disbanded accordingly.

Right: The island platform at Millbrook, where the four-track main line has the fast lines on the outside. Pictured on 17 July 1965, Standard Class 4 4-6-0 No 75068 can thus be assumed to have been on a stopping service from Eastleigh, destined probably for Bournemouth. The sidings to the right were used for docks traffic.

Above left: Before leaving Southampton proper (which, as explained in the Introduction, had its locomotives provided by Eastleigh) we turn our attention to the docks area, which for many years was under railway control and possessed its own running shed. Locomotives from the docks would often find their way to and from Eastleigh, for both overhaul and unscheduled repair, and consequently all of the machines that could be seen within the docks could also be seen in due course at Eastleigh shed. From the east side access to the docks themselves involved crossing Canute Road, which (as no gates were provided) required flagmen, seen here as No 41299 crosses cautiously from Southampton Terminus on 28 May 1966.

Left: Shunting in the docks area was for many years the province of the 'USA' tanks, but it should not be forgotten that there was also a considerable amount of transfer working between the Eastern and Western docks themselves. The 'E4' 0-6-2Ts were regularly used for such workings, No 32106 being so employed when photographed on 16 June 1962.

Above: A minor derailment within the docks on 14 April 1962, involving 'E4' No 32510 and necessitating the attendance of the Eastleigh steam crane. The breakdown gang received an extra allowance whenever their vans were required to leave the Eastleigh shed area, so it is perhaps not surprising to see such a good turnout.

Above: Surprisingly, to the casual visitor, the docks area was not all jetties and cranes, for there were also expanses of well-tended grass. Likewise it was not only the ocean-liner passenger services that penetrated the docks, but more usually the regular freight workings; here, on 17 March 1962, 'S15' 4-6-0 No 30508 arrives at the Eastern Docks with a mixed train under the watchful eye of the South Western Hotel.

Right: A concluding view in the docks alongside '101' berth, as 'E4' 0-6-2T No 32104 pauses in its shunting activities on what is a beautiful summers day, 20 July 1961. Reposing in the background is the *Oxfordshire*.

Above: West now, into the New Forest at Brockenhurst, where on 14 October 1961 un-rebuilt 'West Country' No 34019 *Bideford* has just left the station with the Brighton–Bournemouth through train and is passing 'M7' No 30133 working the Lymington–Brockenhurst local. Eastleigh was responsible for supplying the engines to the small shed at Lymington, although the men were relieved as required from Bournemouth.

Above right: A favourite location for Tony was Lymington Junction where three routes diverged. That to the right went to Lymington Town and Pier, whilst out of view to the left was the 'old road' via Ringwood and Wimborne. Straight ahead, and the course being taken on 14 October 1961 by 'N'-class 2-6-0 No 31818, working hard on the climb to the next station, at Sway, was the 'new' line to Bournemouth.

Right: Freight to Lymington was never considerable in volume and in the main consisted of coal. Such services were worked by Eastleigh men and machines, the latter typified by Standard Class 4 2-6-0 No 76015, seen passing the advertising sign for the local golf club on the single-track branch on 14 October 1961.

73

Passenger working, this time on the main line westwards. 'U'-class 2-6-0 No 31804, with a Bulleid coach set, is steaming well as it starts the climb to Sway. The date is recorded as 14 October 1961, the time 1.27pm.

The westernmost point of our photographic journey is Bournemouth, where Eastleigh-based BR Standard Class 4 2-6-0 No 76007 was recorded on a stopping service to Weymouth on 10 June 1967. The advent of the '76xxx' class at Eastleigh in the early 1950s was not without incident, the first members being considered shy for steam until a minor modification to blastpipe and chimney corrected any problems. After that they were welcomed by drivers and firemen alike, management recognising that some advantage could be gained by allocating one crew to each locomotive, which situation pertained for some years afterwards. Sadly such times were a distant memory by 1967, and No 76007 would be withdrawn with the remaining Southern steam fleet just a few weeks later.

Above left: Returning now to the Eastleigh area, this time a brief glimpse of Eastleigh locomotives working some of the local lines radiating from the station. The first of these was the line to Chandlers Ford and Romsey, illustrated here with 'Battle of Britain' No 34063 *229 Squadron* leaving a wintry Chandlers Ford with the diverted 8.40am Cardiff–Portsmouth on 7 March 1965.

Left: Sunnier times and a busy yard, compared with the defunct sidings seen in the previous view. 'S15' 4-6-0 No 30824 has charge of a Salisbury–Eastleigh freight, on the last leg of its journey on 24 March 1962.

Above: Slightly further west, the Romsey line traversed a public level crossing at Halterworth. Seen here is another 'S15', No 30845, this time with a service for Portsmouth.

With the 'S15s' all withdrawn by 1967, remaining freight and parcels traffic was in the hands of BR Standard and Bulleid machines. An unidentified and somewhat tired-looking '76xxx' Class 4 2-6-0 is seen near Chandlers Ford on 4 July 1967 with a train of vans *en route* from Salisbury to Eastleigh.

Special working at Romsey. Maunsell-designed 'Q'-class 0-6-0 No 30548 arrives with the 'Hampshire Venturer' enthusiasts' special of 18 April 1964. The train had originated at Portsmouth and then paused at Eastleigh, where 'USA' 0-6-0T No 30073 was used to pull the coaches for a works visit; it then continued behind No 30548 to Romsey (as seen here) before visiting Andover Junction, Salisbury, Fordingbridge, Hamworthy, Poole, Ringwood and Southampton.

On the opposite side of Eastleigh was the line through Botley to Fareham and thence to either Gosport or Portsmouth. The Fareham line was also a useful diversionary route; here 'West Country' No 34021 *Dartmoor* takes the Netley path away from the station with a diverted service from Waterloo to Bournemouth on 28 October 1960.